Misogyny

for Beginners

Hard-hitting and thought-provoking poetry

Annie Lloyd-Hyde

First published 2022 by Compass-Publishing UK

ISBN 978-1-912009-96-1

Edited and typeset by A Neater Page

Contact: anne.yeadonpoetry@gmail.com

Dedication

I am fortunate that these poems have not been inspired by personal experience of misogyny.

Many are less fortunate and, for them, surviving violence is a day-to-day reality.

These poems are for them.

Contents

There's No Place Like Home

There's no place like home
No place you'd
Least like to be
A claustrophobic web
Of tension
Unpredictability.
Home.
A trip-wired
Trap-laid
Survival course,
Malice in wonderland
With GBH
Flying words
Flying fists
Frightened mother
Who insists,
"It's only because he cares".

This is the Dawn – Boys Will Be Boys

This is the dawn
Expectations are born
Boys under pressure
To be like a man
Peers never more powerful
Phone ever to hand
A passport to porn
It's another land
They do things differently there.

And "*boys will be boys*"
In it together
Don't bowl
Or run or catch
Like a girl
Don't show soft emotion
Or lips will curl
You're a red-blooded male
Developing banter
You're coming of age.

This is the Dawn – Girls: Super Slim Perfection

Girls know that
This is the dawn
Expectations are spawned
Your phone an appendage
Compulsively checked
Your new alter ego
Clearly reflects
Your new cyber world:
Snapchatting
Instagramming
TikTok
It doesn't stop;
Screen showing
Perfect bodies
Super slim
Happiness
Is being thin
Hunger now the enemy
Vomiting the remedy
For body shape
Perfection.

Denial

I'm 13 and dead lucky
When I'm watching
Porn in my room
My mum respects privacy
And never assumes
She can just barge in.
And if she did
She would die of shock
Seeing a screen
Which would be hot
With choking or slapping
Girls covered in jizz
I'd say, "I'm sorry mum
But that's just how it is".

The Patient Paedophile

Young girl, Anna
13 soon
Phone, clutched tightly
In her bedroom
Cocooned, alone
The family asleep
Drunk her first vodka
Totally neat
She feels happy
Can this be real?

She's met this boy
They met online
Ben, 17
Profile: divine!
Cool, good-looking
But misunderstood
Writes her poems
Makes her feel good.

In reality
It's Barry, 52
Plump face and rosy hue
Who gains his thrills
And happiness
From selfies of young girls
Half-dressed
And Anna
High on vodka and verse
Wants to make him happy, of course.

Breaking You In

The first slap is the sweetest
A testament of power
Intense as desire
Swinging arm
Swinging anger
Slapping climax
Sweet release.

Respect

I don't do predictable
I do bolts-out-of-the-blue
My temper's edgy
Call it wild and free
Don't tell a soul
But I'll take control
So do as you're told
And *Respect*.

Sex Education Lesson
by Sam

Sex education with Mrs Jones
Was a total, total bore
It didn't have any interesting bits
Like on Tom's phone that we saw.

She didn't talk about blow-jobs
That boys should always expect,
It's just politeness really
And shows us a bit of respect.

She didn't mention that girls should be shaved
So it's much more pleasant for us,
That we like to swap pics of their intimate bits
And they enjoy a bit of rough.

Some of the girls are slags or sluts
And virgins – they're the worst
Girls can get angry and emotional
I think it must be 'The Curse'.

Mrs Jones talked about consent
But she really ought to know
That the girls we saw on Tom's phone
Mean 'Yes' when they say 'No'.

Sex Education Lesson
by Samantha

Sex education with Mrs Jones
Was a total waste of time
There was contraception
And other stuff
But not how to react
When boys want it rough
Like they show us
On their phones.

She didn't talk about blow-jobs
That some boys say is their right
The names you're called
The perpetual pressures
The texting, the sexting
Well into the night.

Nothing was mentioned
About shaving down there
The soreness, the rawness
It's just bloody unfair
And, Mrs Jones, being called a virgin
Is no longer something to brag
It's just one of the many names
Like 'Whore' and 'Slut' and 'Slag'.

And when you talked of consent
I think that you might guess
That some boys develop deafness
And mis-hear 'No' for 'Yes'.

Two Worlds

I live in two worlds
So do my mates
My Family World
With the usual stuff –
Homework
Family meals
Doing enough
To get by.

Taken to matches
Sometimes helping my mum
Arguments
Birthday cakes
Then holidays come
Grandpa staying
Telling jokes you've heard
But that's okay
In your Family World.

Then there's Phone World
That belongs to us boys.
My phone and I
Inseparable
X-rated content on tap
Hard in my pocket
Addictive
And no lovey-dovey crap
Pure porn.

There's a wank list
Of options
So you're spoilt for choice –
Oral or anal
Hard-core or rape
Maybe
Choking, groping
Cumming in their face
Or mouth.

Gang Bangs are tempting
Blokes unrelenting
Their roughness arousing
And when they're done
It's your turn to cum
And you're away.

And sometimes I wonder
About the girls who cry
Is it a show or a bluff
And Tom rolls his eyes
And says, "Of course it is.
Don't you know
Girls like it rough?"

Free Kicks

He taught her the footie rules
Using a hands-on approach
And he liked the free kicks best of all.

The Offside Rule

She knows about the Offside Rule
She's been offside for a while
Her once happy Saturdays
Are now 'Slug-and-Slapperdays'
In a 90-minute slot
With added injury time.

The Fairground of Deviant Delights

Roll up!
Roll up!
Roll up and see
What Porn has done
For equality
See the sex act
Like you've never seen before
Intoxicating, violent
With addictive allure
Now the real thing
Seems pedestrian
Predictable
Tame
And any prospective woman
Of mine
Has to up their game.

Bringing You Down

I'll savour bringing you down
Feeling your happiness
Darken and fade
That sparky confidence
Once flying so free
Now a captured bird
Caught in a sea
Of my casual derision.

My caustic comments
Designed to erode
Your self-reliance
Your easy mode
Of being;
Your dress too tight
Your love of food
Seeing your judgement
Distorted, skewed
And friends kept away.

And if I sense you plan to escape
Feel you can take no more,
I'll turn on the charm
Seek your forgiveness
Beg on my knees
As God be my witness
For I'll change, start afresh
I'll pursue and persuade
And be assured
Those bruises will fade.

I Miss Him

I miss him
When he's away
And when he's back
My arms embrace
My traveller has returned
Back to his rightful place
With me.

But there's a subtle shift
I'm sensing unease
Smelling deception
Seeing the wood through the trees
And this bloodhound
Never misses a trick.

So, the switch is thrown
As I imagine the deception
The treachery
The lechery
The secret seduction.

I'm transformed
I'm manic
I am that woman in the attic
And he's a prisoner in the dock
And he knows what he's got
Coming.

The slaps and the punches
The well-planted kicks
The verbal wind-ups
The expressionless flicks
Of derision.

Reduce him
Traduce him
Ignore all his pleas
Then laugh at him
Crying
Crawling round on his knees.

Together

We're in this together now
The Secret Slapping Club
The bruises hidden
Unless I choose
To show them off
To amuse –
Win 'Lad Points'.

Equality

Mum would get fist-swingingly cross
Dad got the worst of it
She said it was for equality
Her dad hit her mum, you see.

Author's Note:

Misandry is a dislike or hatred of men.

Confusingly, it has slightly different definitions, depending on which reference book you use.

On Finding Your Son Watches Porn

Inevitable
Unstoppable
His exposure to porn,
Not yet a teen
But he knows the form
Phones passed around
And you have to conform.

I check with my conscience
Then look at his phone
Find “Gang Bang Girl”
And enter the zone.
A Hogarthian scene
Featuring three grown men
One young girl,
And it’s no easy viewing
Watching the inevitable unfurl.

She’s pushed and shoved
Into their chosen positions
No holes barred
Constant derision
A cavorting circus
A rugby scrum
And no rules apply
A hole in one
Aroused by subjugation

… and it’s on his phone

Welcome to the unofficial Sex Education lesson ...

Resist the bottle
The urge to throttle
To ban TV
Ban all ‘G’s
Then join the
Amish community.

Instead
Seize the moment
Become unshockable
Open-minded
Cool and logical
In control.

Grab your car keys
For the school pick-up
He’s there by the gate
Climbs in with a smile
Still a child
Hard to reconcile
With “Gang Bang Girl”.

You just need to drive
Side by side
No eye contact
Nowhere to hide.

You jump in at the deep end
Tell him what you've seen
Hot emotions cross his face
Fury, disbelief, disgrace
His privacy invaded
A line has been crossed.

I say,
"I wonder if the girl in the porn
Has the luxury of privacy
I wonder if she has a line
That men cross all the time."

He falls silent, turns away.

Drive
Side by side
No eye contact
Nowhere to hide.

I say,
"There's good porn
And bad porn"
(He looks up)
"And if you're a kid
How can you discern?
There is no label on the lid,
So maybe you think
Good sex is a game
With a slap or two
And it's all about you
A power game for one

Your needs
Your conquest –
Your hour has come."

Drive
Side by side
No eye contact
Nowhere to hide.

My son is on the back-foot
Thrown by this reaction
This quite even response
This analysis of the action
And … *good porn*??

Stop at the lights
School girls crossing
Laughing, jostling
Volume high
Bunch of lads
Hormonal magnets
Nonchalant, cool
All online
And teenage life
Shaped by peers and mates
More than ever before.

I say,
"Do you think some boys
Will see it's fantasy
Or will they see it as reality
Relevant, no disparity?"

He says,
"Don't know what's true
Or what's in their minds
But a few of the older boys
Say they get what they want
And if they're shunned
The girls get the brunt
Ostracised
Called a 'Slag' or a …" (he pauses)

I say,
"*C****"
(Never said it before; horrible, but strangely exhilarating)

Drive, drive
Side-by-side
And talking.

I pause for a bit
As if in a dream
Wallow in a stream
Of consciousness
I'm going surreal
I've got his attention.

I say,
"If I were a critic
That film would be slated
Characterisation poor
Narrative weak
Visuals tedious

Poor quality speech
Vocabulary limited
I'm almost sure
There were more than
*Forty "F***s"*
We had to endure
I mean … please!
Hope there's not more to come
Oh, and one of the men had
An oversized bum."

Keep driving
He's shaken but smiling
He gets it.

We're hungry
Head for a drive-in
And on the way
We talk about fantasy
Talk about reality
Talk about brainwashing
And gender equality
Talk about good sex
Even talk about love.

And finally, I ask him
How it came to be on his phone
And therein lies the rub,
He said 'peer pressure'
Join in or you're dead,
Or be known as a
'F***ing K***head'.

And we stop at a drive-through
And we eat and stare out
And we're both sort of okay
And he mumbles, "*Sorry*"
And I say, "*Me too*"
Which seems a bit confusing
But he knows that it's true
And we both choke up a bit
Then we drive home.

And as we park the car
Get the stuff out of the boot
He says, "Mum,
All men aren't w***ers
I mean … look at Dad."

And we laugh.

Author's Note:

This poem was inspired by the work of Goedele Liekens, a Belgium Politician and Television Presenter. She believes that sex education in British schools is out-of-date and used the Channel 4 programme *"Sex in Class"* to campaign for a more relevant approach to be used by schools.

Girls Watching Porn

More girls watching porn
Female equality
Or male dominancy?

Readers Responses

"Wow!! another fabulous collection of raw, powerful, original and very thought provoking poems … I think they would be a great catalyst to start conversations in secondary schools about sex education"

"… you have a rare gift indeed and a very unique and authentic voice"

PC, Educational Psychologist

"This is an important collection. Your form sits well with the content. There is no preaching and yet the message is crystal clear. The variety around one theme is very effective."

HN, Teacher of Creative Writing

"This poetry collection is absolutely stunning."

DP, University Lecturer

"Deep and unflinching and the language and taut rhythm structures mirror the content. And yet, the punchy delivery is softened."

SG, Therapist

'Bringing You Down'

Just before the final print-run of this book, a friend came to me with an envelope. Inside was the following poem she felt she had to write, about an occasion when she had suffered abuse from her partner. She had never spoken of it to anyone, but 'Bringing You Down' had brought back all the memories.

It only happened once ...
The back of the hand
The hand that I had loved
And had loved me
Now
A weapon of ferocity.

Reproduced with the permission of the author